Overcome Dark Thoughts

OVERCOME

DARK THOUGHTS

100 effective tips for negotiating the harsh realities of an anxious life.

Author's Note

You don't have to be intimately acquainted with the joys of catastrophic thinking or the occasional DEFCON Level 1 panic attack to appreciate this collection of mindfulness(ish) quotes, but it would probably help.

Strap in.
Stop thinking.
Start reading.

Cosmic 44

UNCONTROLLABLE RAGE.

BETTER OUT THAN IN.

Mindfulness is all about finding and focusing on the present moment.

Do not dwell on the past.

Especially if you were happier and more successful in the past.

- [x] It's easy to forget important
- [x] tasks we need to accomplish
- [x] in order to thrive. So, make
- [x] a daily list of these tasks and
- [ ] cross them off one by one as
- [ ] you forget to do them.

Don't let your imposter syndrome fool you.

The **fight, flight** or **freeze** response is your mind and body's natural way of reacting to moments of extreme fear. But a better option is to **faint**. Because a temporary loss of consciousness is way more dignified than getting your butt kicked, running away screaming or shitting your pants.

Unleash your overactive mind.

Because
false hope
is better than
no hope.

Know the difference between good stress and bad stress. Good stress helps you overcome obstacles and perform better, at job interviews or on first dates for example. Whereas bad stress puts you in a constant state of threat and inadequacy, at job interviews or on first dates, for example.

You can't hold back the waves, but you **can** learn to surf. Although it takes years and years of practice, and you need to be quite ripped.

Try to build a positive relationship with your mental suffering. Think of paranoia or anxiety as a lifelong friend who's always got your back and will <u>never</u> let you down.

LETTING GO IS ONE OF THE KEY ASPECTS TO MANAGING STRESS.

SO, JUST LET GO.

OF UNPAID UTILITY BILLS AND VEHICLE TAX.

OF PERSONAL GROOMING AND HYGIENE.

OF YOUR DREAMS AND RESPONSIBILITIES.

JUST FUCK IT ALL.

TRY STIMULATING YOUR BRAIN WITH A SERIES OF
MENTAL GYMNASTICS DESIGNED TO PUSH YOU
OUT FROM YOUR COMFORT ZONE.

LIKE SEX WITH A RANDOM STRANGER

OR CLIMBING A TREE FOR NO
DISCERNIBLE REASON.

OR SHOPLIFTING.

Focus on the **PUDDLE** of positives.

Not the OCEAN of negatives.

DON'T PLACE TOO MUCH EMPHASIS
ON YOUR PRODUCTIVITY.
FOCUS ON CONSUMPTION.
BINGE ON FAST FOOD AND CANDY
BARS, CAFFEINE AND MILKSHAKES, TV
SHOWS AND VIDEO GAMES.
TIME ENJOYED IS NOT TIME WASTED.

Stop judging others. It's not their fault they're more successful than you are.

Take a moment to wonder at the stars shining in the sky each night to ground yourself and put problems into perspective. Remember you are no more than a smudge on a speck of dust, idly drifting within a sterile cosmic void measuring approximately ninety-five billion light years in diameter.

Lighten up a bit.

66

Checking emails last thing at night and the moment you wake up in the morning is a great way to centre a restless mind.

99

Write a 'To Don't' list to help
add structure to your day.

Don't leave your house.

Don't answer the front door.

Don't open any mail.

Don't watch daytime news.

You'll soon perk up.

If someone buys you a mindful journal for you to write your anxious thoughts and feelings down in, make a note in it to *never speak to them again.*

TO MAXIMIZE
PRODUCTIVITY WORK IN
TEN-MINUTE BLOCKS,
WITH SIXTY-MINUTE
INTERVALS TO RECOVER
AND REFUEL.

**Practice positive self-talk as often as you can.
Use affirmations to strengthen your
mindset and build self-esteem.**

"Catastrophizing is good for me".

"9 am the king of catastrophizing".

And so forth.

GET AWAY FROM IT
ALL AND GO ON A
MINDFULNESS RETREAT.

YOU'RE BOUND TO
DISCOVER NEW THINGS
ABOUT YOURSELF AS
WELL AS OTHER PEOPLE
EVEN MORE FUCKED UP
THAN YOU ARE.

DON'T BE HELD HOSTAGE
BY ANXIETY.

ALWAYS TRY TO NEGOTIATE
YOURSELF AWAY FROM NEGATIVE
THOUGHTS PEACEFULLY BEFORE
AMBUSHING THEM WITH MULTIPLE
PRECISION VODKA SHOTS.

Be a worrier, not a warrior.

Worriers seek safety and comfort whereas
warriors seek danger and risk.

Worriers live longer than warriors.

Always start your day with some light breathing exercises
to help channel and organize your thoughts.

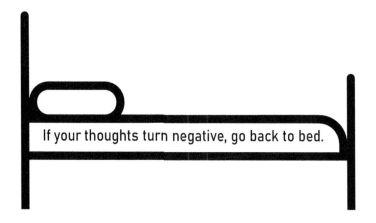

If your thoughts turn negative, go back to bed.

Rejoice in the ordinary things.

Like a perfectly
timed poached egg
or discovering you're
only tenth in the
queue as you wait
to speak to a doctor
on the phone for a
medical emergency.

Turn the tables on your intrusive thoughts. They don't all have to be negative. If you catch yourself thinking about your cheating ex and their new partner, imagine them suffocating together adrift in the empty vacuum of space.

Lungs ruptured. Eyes boiled. Their naked bodies ballooned up to twice their normal size.

And freezing to death.

What doesn't kill you will keep trying until it does.

Like the T-1000 in *Terminator 2: Judgement Day*.

The most effective way to lower a racing heartbeat is to go into cardiac arrest.

Choose a specific goal and tell a friend what it is, how you will achieve it and by when.

Making this goal public means you will be more motivated to succeed.

If you fail to achieve your goal, tell your friend

TO KEEP THEIR BIG FUCKING MOUTH SHUT.

PHYSICAL TOUCH IS KEY TO EASING ANXIETY AS IT PROMOTES THE RELEASE OF OXYTOCIN, A HORMONE ASSOCIATED WITH HAPPINESS AND LOWER STRESS LEVELS. SO, NEVER MISS AN OPPORTUNITY TO HUG SOMEONE.

EVEN IF YOU HAVE COVID-19.

Laughter is not the best medicine.

Alprazolam and Diazepam are.

Don't stress about the things you cannot change.

Stress about the things you *can* change but you're failing spectacularly to do so.

Any time you start a sentence with
"*I will*"
or
"*I shall*",
change it to
"*I might*".

This changes your perspective and
intentions on things and offers you an
escape route from chores like going to the
gym or meeting friends for dinner.

It's important to remember you can always take a step back from any stressful situation.

Just be mindful of fresh dog turds.

Hard work and diligence are the enemies of procrastination.

If you're experiencing a severe panic attack, calm yourself by sitting in a comfortable chair and writing down a list of all the people who've wronged you in the past. Focus on some rather creative and brutal ways you will take revenge.

Never underestimate the healing powers of a Big Mac.

Jesus proved his divine nature by turning water into wine. Blessed are his many disciples who wander the road to nowhere, numbing the pain of their aimless lives as they go, through the holy gift of alcohol.

Praise Jesus!

The greatest weapon we have against anxiety is our ability to choose which particular **trigger** will be the one that finally cracks us open like a stuffed piñata at a Mexican wedding on Cinco de Mayo.

Gardening is good for the
mind and body.

Grow your own soil.

Tend to your own flowers.

Piss on your own weeds.

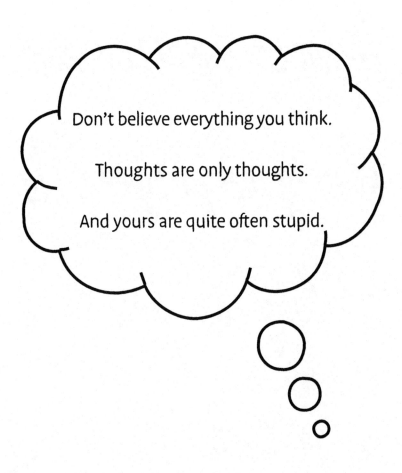

Don't believe everything you think.

Thoughts are only thoughts.

And yours are quite often stupid.

It doesn't matter how slow your progress is as long as you turn up on time.

EMBRACE DEMENTIA ONCE IT SETS IT.

For there will no longer be such things as Guy Ritchie movies.

66

Aim to do one good deed each day.

And five relatively bad ones.

99

Professional networking events and direct messages on social media are great ways to connect with mentors who can help to motivate and inspire. Gain as many valuable life lessons and insights as you can before they place restraining orders on you.

Worrying about problems is a futile enterprise. Most cannot be solved so just ignore them.

They'll go away on their own eventually.

HAVING A HEALTHY MIND IS JUST AS IMPORTANT AS HAVING A COOL WARDROBE.

Live each moment as if it's your last.

Just in case.

THE NEXT TIME YOU INTERACT WITH SOMEONE, TAKE NOTE
OF THREE THINGS ABOUT THEM.

DOES THEIR BREATH SMELL?

IS ONE EYE LARGER THAN THE OTHER?

CAN YOU COUNT THE WRINKLES ON THEIR FOREHEAD?

IMPROVING YOUR FOCUS PROMOTES CELL GROWTH AND
BOOSTS BRAIN POWER, WHICH YOU CAN THEN USE TO MAKE
POSITIVE AFFIRMATIONS ABOUT YOURSELF.

Let go of the people you are attached to.

↘→ Attachments lead to suffering.

↘→ Suffering leads to pain.

↘→ Pain leads to death.

↘→ Death leads to a funeral.

↘→ A funeral leads to a wake.

↘→ Which leads to more attachments.

We live in a technological world where a diverse range of mobile apps now offer unlimited emotional support to keep you calm or distracted in a time of crisis.

VEGAS JACKPOT PARTY,

ESCAPE OR DIE

and

TINDER

are particularly effective.

You will never land. You can only f
a
l
l.

The Emotional Freedom Technique
<EFT> restores balance to your body
by triggering its energy hot spots.
Repeated finger tapping across your
scalp, eyebrows, under your nose and
on your chin may look absurd but
remember, most people think you're
bonkers anyway.

You alone are *enough.*

You have nothing to prove to *anyone.*

Except your *mother.*

FAILURE IS NOT A DIRTY WORD.

IS A DIRTY WORD.

Just breathe.

Note how your breath feels as you inhale through
your nose and exhale through your mouth.

Well done.

Not that hard, is it.

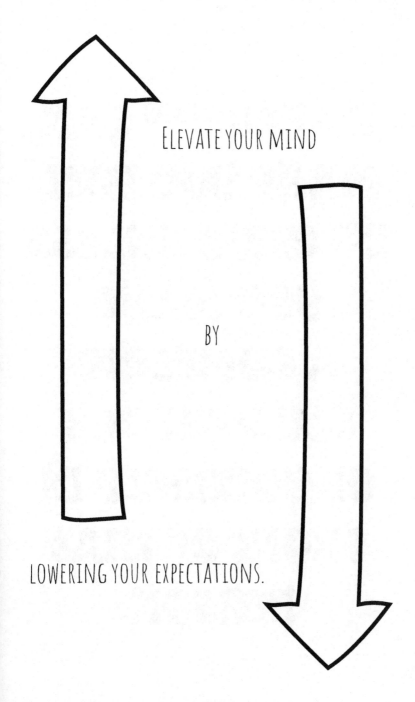

Elevate your mind

by

lowering your expectations.

NO PERSON CAN
MAKE YOU FEEL
INFERIOR UNLESS
YOU MAKE
A COMPLETE
CLUSTERFUCK
OF YOURSELF IN
FRONT OF THAT
PERSON.

Never put off until tomorrow
what should be done today.
Put it off until next week
or the week after because
tomorrow is already jammed.

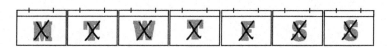

Regularly practicing
meditation and yoga will
lead to you regularly
practicing
sexual intercourse.

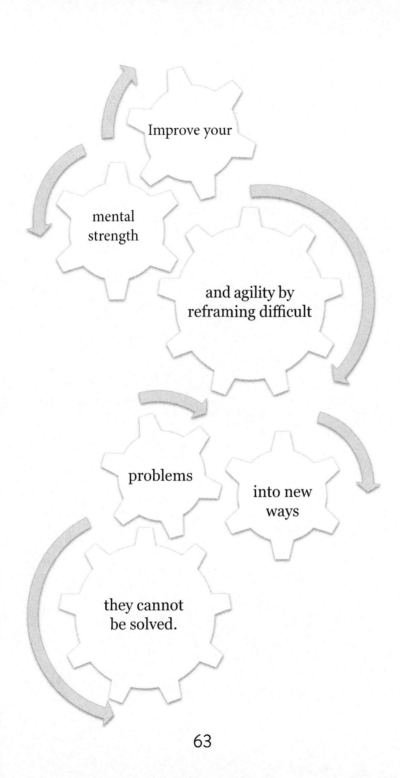

Improve your mental strength and agility by reframing difficult problems into new ways they cannot be solved.

ALWAYS TRY TO FOSTER A POSITIVE AND HEALTHY MIND IN THE WORKPLACE.

AVOID TAKING WORK HOME WITH YOU BY NOT GOING TO WORK AT ALL.

LET YOUR INNER VOICE
GUIDE YOU AS MUCH AS
IT WANTS BUT CONSIDER
GETTING A SECOND OPINION.

Avoid taking cold showers and people who advocate for the benefits of cold-water therapy.

These people are liars, frauds and masochists.

It's your life.
Take ownership of it.
You are the writer of your
own screenplay. Just stop
giving your screenplay to
M Night Shyamalan.

Micro-workouts offer anxious people quick ways to boost confidence and keep fit at home. A structured routine of **blinking reps, smiling crunches, mobile phone curls and remote-control leg lifts** can all help to release tension and should be rewarded with a *deep tissue massage* complete with a selection of soothing aromatherapy oils.

The difference between a good
psychotherapist and a bad one
is around ninety pounds sterling.

Paradise is not a state
of consciousness. It's
a tropical beach in the
Bahamas.

You don't have to suffer perpetual chaos in order to grow and learn as a human being. But it will give you a massive advantage.

LUCK IS THE RESULT OF AN UNLIKELY CHAIN OF IMPROBABLE EVENTS. IT DOES NOT COME FROM HARD WORK.

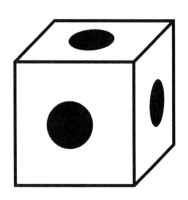

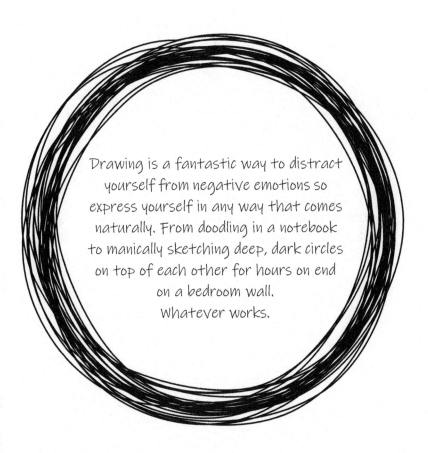

Drawing is a fantastic way to distract
yourself from negative emotions so
express yourself in any way that comes
naturally. From doodling in a notebook
to manically sketching deep, dark circles
on top of each other for hours on end
on a bedroom wall.
Whatever works.

Invest in a good mattress. You'll be spending at least three quarters of your life on it so make it count.

We cannot force mindfulness upon ourselves. We can only try to force it upon others.

NEVER GO RED WITH
EMBARRASSMENT.

IT'S A SIGN OF
WEAKNESS.

INSTEAD, TRY TO
DEVELOP ROSACEA.

CALM AN
ANXIOUS MIND
WITH
THOUGHTS
THAT
YOU
ARE
HOPEFULLY
LIVING
IN A
SIMULATION
LAND
NOTHING
AND NO-ONE
IS
REAL

Practicing sleep hygiene allows an overactive mind time to repair and recharge. To ensure a deep and undisturbed night's sleep invest in a strict bedtime ritual involving light yoga, a hot foot bath, some mindful colouring, guided meditation and a cup of warm milk. Or just turn off the lights and masturbate like a normal person.

A game-changing new study by the
Karolinska Institute in Stockholm suggests
you can cure yourself of social anxiety by
sniffing other people's armpit sweat.

No, but like seriously.

A YEAR FROM NOW EVERYTHING YOU'RE STRESSING ABOUT SIMPLY WON'T MATTER.

They'll be a whole bunch of new shit to deal with.

Never forget to celebrate achieving daily goals and personal accomplishments, such as waving to someone across the street or smiling at yourself in the mirror.

FIND QUIET, EMPTY
SPACES TO PRACTICE YOUR
MINDFULNESS.

LIKE A BENCH IN A
NEIGHBOURHOOD PARK

OR ANY BRANCH OF
WH SMITH.

Avoid waking up on the wrong side of the bed by sleeping on the sofa.

Flex your biceps and lift your shoulders towards your ears.

Take a deep breath through your nose and hold it for a count of thirty.

Now make tight fists with your hands, tilt your head to the left but let your eyes look to the right.

Hold this pose for another count of thirty.

Finally, release, relax and call yourself an ambulance.

Setting healthy boundaries that limit
physical and emotional interaction with
others is an important part of self-care.

Where possible, reinforce these
boundaries with a mix of tripwires,
electric fences and landmines.

SURROUND YOURSELF WITH WINNERS.

DITCH THE DEAD- BEATS.

"ONE STRATEGY TO GAIN CONTROL OVER
ANXIETY IS TO ALLOW YOURSELF TO
RUMINATE NEGATIVE THOUGHTS IN YOUR
HEAD REPEATEDLY FOR A SET PERIOD
OF TIME EACH DAY, TYPICALLY NO MORE
THAN TWELVE HOURS."

IF YOU CAN'T BEAT
THEM, JOIN THEM.

AND THWART THEIR
HOPES AND DREAMS
COVERTLY FROM
THE INSIDE UNTIL
THEY'RE LEFT IN RUINS
WONDERING WHAT THE
FUCK HIT THEM.

THEN LEAVE.

TRY MAKING A SELF-SOOTHE BOX
CONTAINING ITEMS THAT CALM, GROUND
OR DISTRACT YOU DURING PERIODS OF
PANIC.

A JAFFA CAKE. A PACK OF INDOOR
FIREWORKS. PICTURES OF DOGS. CASH.

THAT KIND OF THING.

Bribery will get you everywhere.

Doing absolutely nothing with your life is technically still doing a little bit of something.

Scrape the bottom of the barrel until you find the **trap**door.

NEVER THINK YOU ARE TOO OLD TO
CHALLENGE YOURSELF AND MASTER A
NEW SKILL, BUT DON'T BOTHER TRYING
TO CODE OR LEARN MANDARIN.

SHIPS LIKE THOSE HAVE SAILED WAY
BEYOND YOUR HORIZON.
STICK TO BAKING.

"

Share your wisdom.

Help others to avoid the social traps
and mental pitfalls you've managed to
effortlessly cartwheel straight in to.

Close your eyes and take a long, deep breath.

It's just been a bad few years.

THE BEST WAY TO
CAPTURE THE ESSENCE
OF LIFE IS TO TAKE
HEED OF ITS SUBTLE
SIGNALS.

THAT GRINNING
TRAFFIC WARDEN.

THE COUGHING BUM
ASKING FOR CHANGE.

A HOODY CLENCHING
A SWITCHBLADE IN
HIS POCKET.

PAY ATTENTION!

Sixteen hours of meditation a day can

really help to ease an anxious mind.

Try keeping a stress journal.
On each page write down dates,
times, places and thoughts that
contribute to you feeling stressed.
Then tear these pages out and
wipe your arse with them.

Love yourself.

You are brilliant and unique.

You are bold and confident.

You look fabulous and are an amazing human being.

Act like you're the biggest narcissist on the planet.

THERE IS NO MAGIC PILL THAT CAN SOLVE YOUR PROBLEMS FOR YOU.

AT LEAST, NOT A LEGAL ONE.

TO ENSURE MENTAL WELL-BEING, IT'S ESSENTIAL TO SEPARATE YOUR

THOUGHTS FROM YOUR IDENTITY. YOUR THOUGHTS DO NOT DEFINE YOU.

JUST BECAUSE YOU'RE THINKING OF JAMES CORDEN SPONTANEOUSLY

COMBUSTING LIVE ON TV DOESN'T MAKE YOU A BAD PERSON. IT'S

JUST A THOUGHT, AND MOST PEOPLE HAVE THOUGHTS LIKE THESE.

THERE IS NO FUTURE.

THERE IS NO PAST.

THERE IS NO PRESENT.

THERE IS NOTHING.

EXCEPT MINDFULNESS.

AND QUOTES ABOUT MINDFULNESS.

Afterword

Only the bravest of the brave reach the end of this book.
You hung in there and you made it.
You overcame dark thoughts. Congratulations.

But if I may be serious for a brief moment...

Whatever's happening in your life just keep moving.
Keep walking the path. Wherever it's taking you. One
foot in front of the other. As tall as you can. Don't stop.
No looking back. Only forward. Just keep moving. Until
you're where you need to be. Where you belong.

You'll know it when you get there.
And everything will be just fine.

Cosmic 44

OVERCOME

DARKER
THOUGHTS

Another 100 effective tips to negotiate the harsh realities of an anxious life if the previous 100 effective tips proved ineffective.

Overcoming Soon

ACCEPT

DARK THOUGHTS

100 effective tips to pull you back from the swirling vortex of mental oblivion and finally turn that anxious frown upside down.

Succumbing Soon

Printed in Great Britain
by Amazon

23538635R00064